The Abbey and Palace of Dunfermline

Richard Fawcett

*Principal Inspector of Ancient Monuments,
Historic Buildings and Monuments*

Published by HISTORIC SCOTLAND (Historic Buildings and Monuments)
Edited by Christopher Tabraham.
Designed by The Marketing & Design Agency Ltd.
and typeset by Artwork Associates.
Principal photography by David Henrie.
Drawings by Harry Bland.
Printed in Scotland by Holmes McDougall Ltd.

The Prospect of y^e Town & Abby of DUMFERMLING.

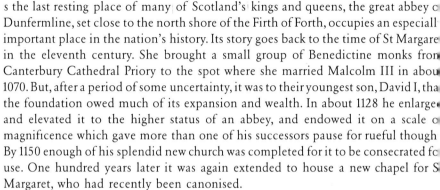

The Abbey and Palace of Dunfermline

As the last resting place of many of Scotland's kings and queens, the great abbey of Dunfermline, set close to the north shore of the Firth of Forth, occupies an especially important place in the nation's history. Its story goes back to the time of St Margaret in the eleventh century. She brought a small group of Benedictine monks from Canterbury Cathedral Priory to the spot where she married Malcolm III in about 1070. But, after a period of some uncertainty, it was to their youngest son, David I, that the foundation owed much of its expansion and wealth. In about 1128 he enlarged and elevated it to the higher status of an abbey, and endowed it on a scale of magnificence which gave more than one of his successors pause for rueful thought. By 1150 enough of his splendid new church was completed for it to be consecrated for use. One hundred years later it was again extended to house a new chapel for St Margaret, who had recently been canonised.

1

Apart from St Margaret and David I, the monarch most associated with the abbey in the popular mind is Robert I (the Bruce), who was buried before its high altar in 1329. Robert was also a benefactor of the monks after their domestic buildings had been destroyed by the English in 1303. The interest of successive monarchs in the abbey, the burial place of their ancestors, was further sustained because it frequently provided them with accommodation. Hospitality to the family of its founder was an essential function of a religious house and it is likely that the great guest house, which still stands in a ruined state, was in essence a royal residence from the time of its construction.

The religious life of the abbey came to an abrupt end with the Reformation in 1560. The nave of its church, though, continued to serve as a parish kirk for the townsfolk until 1821. Royal occupation of the guest house was also revived following James VI's grant of the abbey to his queen, Anne of Denmark, in 1589, and it was extensively remodelled to provide her with a handsome palace. Here in 1600 she gave birth to the future Charles I for whom it was last put into repair, in the 1630s.

As Crown property the remains of the abbey church and monastic buildings are now cared for by Historic Buildings and Monuments on behalf of the Secretary of State for Scotland.

X. Malcolme 3 surnamed Canmoir
Began his Rawne, 1057
He maried Margaret dochter to
Edward ye outlaw sone of Edward
yronsyd Kmy of England and wer
buryed at dunfermline

Malcolme 3 . Margaret Quene

2

3

1. The abbey seal *c* 1200.

2. King Malcolm III and Queen
   Margaret, from the 16th-century
   *Seton Armorial. (Sir David
   Lindsay and The National Library
   of Scotland)*

3. King Robert the Bruce, painted
   by George Jamesone in 1633.
   (Private Collection)

Overleaf: A view by Captain John
   Slezer in 1678.

Queen Margaret and the First Church

The early history of Dunfermline is unknown. The 'dun' part of the name could suggest there was an early fortified settlement in the area. By the late eleventh century, it must have been a settlement of some importance – presumably with a royal residence – for in about 1070 King Malcolm III (1058-93) chose it as the place where he would marry Margaret, the refugee Saxon Princess.

Margaret's affection for the place in which she was married was so great that she determined to set up a religious community there. At her request Archbishop Lanfranc of Canterbury sent Goldwine and two other Benedictine monks to form the core of this small priory dedicated to Christ Church and the Holy Trinity. In doing this Margaret was almost certainly attempting to show the Scottish Church something of the more developed forms of monastic life which by then prevailed elsewhere in Europe. However, Margaret's foundation at Dunfermline may be seen as exceptional amongst her many acts of piety in her adoptive country, since in other ways she showed some fondness for the traditions of the Scottish Church as she found it.

Fragments of a church which almost certainly includes Margaret's building were found below the nave in 1916. They have been marked out on the floor with brass strips and are partly visible through grilles in the floor. The evidence was not conclusive, but what was found indicated two phases of building: a tower-nave and choir, to which were added a larger choir with a semi-circular apse for the high altar. It may be that the later eastern parts were additions to the church first built by Margaret. We know that more monks were sent to Dunfermline from Canterbury by St Anselm between 1100 and 1107, possibly because the original community had ceased to exist in the troubles which followed the deaths of Malcolm and Margaret, and this perhaps led to a need for greater accommodation. However, it could be that the earlier part of the building was already in existence at the time of Malcolm and Margaret's marriage, and that they simply added to it to provide a choir for the monks, along with a more suitable setting for the high altar. A mason named Aelric may have been responsible for building, for one Aelric is mentioned in documents relating to the abbey's lands.

1

1. Queen Margaret, from a late-medieval prayer book. *(The University of Edinburgh)*

2. Two pages from Queen Margaret's own Gospel Book. *(The Bodleian Library, Oxford, MS.Lat.Liturg.f.5, folio 30 verso)*

3. Saint Benedict of Nursia. *(Rome, Biblioteca Apostolica Vaticana, MS.Vat.Lat, 1202, f.2r)*

SCS IOHANNES
EUANGELISTA

INCIPITEU
CUNT

IN

CII

uerbum · f
r dni · æd sē
Hoc erat i
Omnia pe
& sine ipso f
factum est · ·
erat lux hom
bris luc&. d
comprehend
miffuf adeo
iohannef · H
um · ut teft
r& delumi
derent per :

Benedictine Monasticism

Following the foundation of Iona by St Columba in AD 565, Scotland had played a distinguished part in the spread of the form of monasticism practised by the monks of the Irish Church.

3

Yet, by the time of Margaret and Malcolm's marriage in about 1070, true monastic life within their country was almost defunct. Elsewhere in Europe, the pattern for monasticism down the rest of the Middle Ages had long been set by a rule of life compiled in about 530 by the abbot of Monte Cassino in southern Italy, St Benedict of Nursia. A particular significance of Margaret's foundation at Dunfermline was that it appears to have been the first community in Scotland to be organised according to this Benedictine rule.

2

King David I and Dunfermline

avid I was the sixth and youngest of Malcolm and Margaret's sons, and the third and last to succeed to the throne. He was an intensely pious monarch, who was also devoted to the memory of his mother. He bestowed great wealth on the small priory in which his parents and elder brothers were buried. (Later kings buried here were Malcolm IV, Alexander I and Robert I.) He had succeeded to the throne in 1124, and by about 1128 his plans for making the house into a major abbey, which might also continue to serve as a worthy burial place for Scotland's royal family, were reaching fruition. Again he looked to Canterbury for guidance, and in 1128 Geoffrey, the prior there, became Dunfermline's first abbot.

Rebuilding of the abbey church on a much grander scale must have begun about the same time. The eastern part, containing the high altar and most of the monks' choir, has been destroyed, but it probably consisted of a limb of three bays, flanked by aisles, and terminating in semi-circular projections known as apses for the high altar and the chapels at the aisle ends. The monks' choir stalls would have extended from the eastern limb to below the tower which rose at the junction of the main body of the church and the laterally extending arms known as transepts. To the west of the tower and transepts is the major surviving part of the medieval church, a nave of eight bays, seven of which were used by the local layfolk as their parish church. The west front of the abbey, which contained the principal processional entrance, was emphasised by a pair of towers above the western bays of the aisles.

1

Dunfermline was planned as a very much bigger and more architecturally splendid building than anything then standing in Scotland, even if not on the vast scale of many of the great new English churches. Other abbey churches on a similar scale, though, were soon to be started under the king's direction. To design and build these great new churches masons had to be brought up from England, since Scottish craftsmen as yet had no experience of raising such complex buildings. David I himself knew Norman England well, having spent part of his earlier adult life at the court of his brother-in-law, Henry I, where he married a Norman heiress, before succeeding to the throne. The breadth of his architectural knowledge is clearly evident in the range of churches erected for him.

At Dunfermline the masons designing the earlier stages of the building operations almost certainly came from Durham, possibly because the death of Bishop Flambard of Durham in 1128 had halted the construction work there. But Dunfermline is no mere copy of Durham, and elements inspired by buildings possibly as far away as Waltham in Essex may be detected.

To ensure the firm foundation of the enlarged community at Dunfermline David immediately bestowed benefactions upon it, including lands in Fife and Midlothian, portions of the royal income, and more exotic endowments such as a proportion of

fica eft fup rivam fluminis wede. in loco at
2

the seals taken at Kinghorn. By the time of his death in 1153 yet more endowments had been granted, including half ownership of the Queensferry passage across the Forth. Others who wished to share in the merit of supporting the prayers of the monks also contributed. By the time of the Reformation Dunfermline was the third richest monastery in Scotland. A favourite means of providing funds for the monastic community was by granting a parish church and its teinds, or tithes. David I began by granting the parishes of Perth and Dunfermline itself. A further twenty-five churches followed although in about seven cases the endowment may have been ineffective.

David's support of Dunfermline was such that it was certain to thrive, and by 1150 enough of the new church was completed for it to be consecrated. By this date it is likely that only the monks' choir was finished and roofed, and the lowest storey of the nave was probably well advanced. The upper storeys of the nave were eventually raised in a simpler manner than the arcades and flanking aisles which supported them, which suggests they were built in a greater hurry and with less resources than the first parts of the structure.

David may also have been responsible for the foundation of the royal burgh of Dunfermline, since he appeared to refer to it as being his own. However, this settlement, which was perhaps on the far side of the burn from the abbey, had only a brief life. It was the prosperous burgh which grew up around the walls of the abbey itself, and under the protection of its abbot, which formed the basis of the later town.

The Abbey's Early Years

1. A cellarer testing the quality of his stocks of wine.

2. A religious community at prayer in their church.
   (The British Library)

3. A Benedictine monk at work.

Organisation

Because of its vast possessions and great wealth, Dunfermline occupied an important position in the social and political structure of the kingdom. Its head, the abbot, was an important lord. In 1245 the status of Dunfermline's abbot was further enhanced when Pope Innocent IV granted him the right to wear the mitre, putting him on an equal footing with a bishop. Beneath the abbot the complex organisation of the abbey required many other office holders. These may have eventually involved up to half the community. They included the prior and sub-prior, to assist with the general administration, and the cellarer, responsible for the abbey's provisions (his stores usually took up much of the west range of the cloister). Amongst others there were the novice master, in charge of new recruits, the almoner, who dispensed charity, the sacrist, who controlled items used in church services, and the infirmarian who looked after old and sick monks.

In its early days the abbey was a highly active institution. A dependent priory was established at Urquhart, near Elgin in Moray, by the 1130s. Before 1153 some of its monks are found further north at Dornoch (in the county of Sutherland, but the diocese of Caithness). Andrew, a former monk of Dunfermline, was bishop there, and it is possible that attempts were being made to form a monastic cathedral establishment there, with Dunfermline as its model.

The first stage of Dunfermline's history as an abbey perhaps ended with the death of Abbot Geoffrey in 1154. But the Canterbury connection continued when his nephew, another Geoffrey, was elected in his place. Royal patronage also continued, and in 1165 David I's grandson and successor, Malcolm IV, was buried in the church.

Later kings laid great store on the abbey for guidance in spiritual matters. According to tradition, in 1199 Malcolm's brother and successor, William the Lion, passed the night at St Margaret's tomb before a projected invasion of England. It was there that he was dissuaded in a dream from making the attack.

No institution can live perpetually on an elevated plane, however, and by 1230 the peace of the abbey was being disturbed by the violent actions of certain monks. It was one of the dilemmas of medieval monasticism that the wealth which their spirituality attracted, from those who wished to make amends for their own sins, made that very spirituality increasingly difficult to maintain.

1

The Daily Round

Although other functions came to be associated with monastic foundations, such as practical charity, hospitality and education, their prime purpose was seen as creating beacons of prayer in a sinful world. To this end there was a perpetual round of services starting at about half past one in the morning, and extending at intervals until the monks retired to their dormitory soon after eight o'clock in the evening. Each day there were seven services known as the Work of God or the 'Hours'. They were made up of psalms, anthems, prayers and readings.

3

The Hours were interspersed with celebrations of the mass and other services according to the time of year and the importance of the particular day in the calendar. After the first of these masses the community met in a room adjacent to the church, known as the chapter house, to discuss the business of the abbey, to read a chapter from the rule of St Benedict (from which the room took its name) and to confess misdemeanours.

2

The Nave of the Abbey Church

f the great abbey church started in about 1128 the only surviving part is the nave, the part open to lay folk and which served as their parish church. As with all major churches of its period it is three storeys in height. At the lowest level a tall arcade carried on cylindrical piers opens into the flanking aisles; at the middle level is the gallery corresponding to the roof space above the aisles; at the top is the clearstorey the windows of which cast light into the central part of the nave.

Internally the arcade and aisles are designed in a grand manner which shows many detailed similarities with the comparable work on the nave of Durham Cathedral Dunfermline, though, was only half its size. The piers at the eastern end of the nave are particularly emphasised by spiralling or zig-zag patterns in a way which is found at several contemporary churches, including Durham; here at Dunfermline this

1

2

3

decoration was probably intended to draw attention to the main nave altar for the lay folk, which was situated between them. All of the piers have caps of scalloped pattern. In the aisles the stone vaults which cover them spring from the piers and from triplets of corresponding shafts along the outer walls. Between these shafts are windows with zig-zag decorated arches above a decorative wall arcade carried on paired shafts.

4

1. The stone vaults over the aisles.
2. A triplet wall shaft in the aisle.
3. The nave looking west.
4. The abbey church as it may have looked when completed in the late 12th century.

1

2

By contrast the upper storeys appear rather plain. The gallery arches have just a single shaft and arch moulding at the wall centre, whilst the severity of the clearstorey stage is only slightly reduced by an angle shaft on each side of the openings on the inner side of the wall passage. Drawings from the eighteenth and nineteenth centuries suggest that the upper parts of the first phase of work (which extended into the east bay of the nave where there were the screen walls closing off the monks' choir) were of comparable richness with the lower parts. The gallery and clearstorey of the main part of the nave thus seem to have been finished off in an inferior way indicating that once the eastern limb and the nave aisles had been completed, money was less readily available. The death of David I in 1153, and the resumption of work on Durham with the consequent recall of the masons who had worked there, could both have contributed to this. In some respects the detail of the upper parts is closer to that in the fragmentary nave of Carlisle Cathedral than to Durham, and it could be that masons from there were brought up to finish the work.

Externally the abbey nave is now partly obscured by the massive arched buttresses which were built against its aisles in the 1620s. But, as with the interior, the lower parts were more finely finished than the upper. The aisles were divided into bays by strip-like pilaster buttresses, between which the windows were framed by zig-zag arches or nook shafts. At gallery level there was a great deal of reconstruction in the 1840s when the outer walls were rebuilt to their original height, but most of the windows appear to have had paired openings. They now have triangular heads, although it is uncertain if this reflects their earlier appearance. The clearstorey windows are treated as round headed apertures with the simplest of framing mouldings.

3

Surviving features indicate something of the way in which the nave was used. The grand processional entrance was in the west front, between the two towers. It was framed by five orders of arches carried on detached shafts. On the north side was the entrance for the lay folk, a smaller version of the west door, with only four orders of arches. In most monastic churches there were two doorways from the cloister for the monks. These usually faced down the east and west walks so that the monks could pass around the whole complex on their Sunday procession. But at Dunfermline there was originally only one door, part way down the north cloister walk rather than at the junction of the north and east walks. However, as befitted the monks' chief entrance to the church, this door has the finest carving to be found in the abbey. It is unusually well preserved, because it was later covered by a burial vault. (This vault may have been built by Queen Anne of Denmark, but in 1616 it was passed to the Wardlaw family, and was partly demolished in 1905.) The capitals of the doorway are carved with exquisite foliage carving ultimately inspired by classical prototypes, and which would originally have been richly painted. It is clearly the work of one of the best of the masons who had come from Durham. Other examples of his work may still be seen there.

The monks' choir was separated from the nave by two screen walls rising to perhaps a third of the total height of the interior. The eastern of these was the pulpitum, which would have had a central doorway; to the west of this was the rood screen, so called from the rood or crucifix placed above it. The lower part of the rood screen still survives, and traces may be seen of the two doors which pierced it. The nave altar stood between these doors. The Sunday procession of the monks paused in front of it before passing into the choir. Parts of the screens across the aisles are also to be seen below the later masonry.

5

4

1. The upper storeys.

2. The south-east doorway.

3. The west doorway.

4. The south doorway.

5. A detail of the carved capitals of the south doorway.

1

2

Later Alterations to the Nave

The nave has undergone a number of alterations over the years. In the time of Abbot Richard de Bothwell (1446-82) the north-west corner of the nave had to be rebuilt, and the eight-lobed arcade pier at that point is his work; on the aisle wall opposite this pier the keen-eyed may spot where he removed the original vaulting shafts. Bothwell also rebuilt the lower part of the tower and added the finely-vaulted porch giving protection to the lay folk's entrance on the north side. His work is identified by his own arms, and also by the bogus arms which came to be associated with St Margaret in the later Middle Ages. It may have been about the same time as these operations that three larger traceried windows were inserted in the north aisle and a single large window placed in the west front. (It was easier to enlarge the windows in the north aisle than in the south, since there was no cloister on that side to restrict the lowering of the sills.) The other windows were retained in their twelfth-century form, although they were probably slightly widened by paring down the surrounding splay. On the west front there is evidence that the new window involved the removal of two tiers of three round-headed windows above the processional door.

Other late-medieval alterations included the formation of a second doorway from the cloister, towards the west end of the south aisle. This presumably made the processions of the monks easier to organise on the orthodox pattern. One of the most interesting items from this period is the sixteenth-century painting on the vault above the eastern bay of the north aisle. A saint appears on each quarter of the vault, and the names of Peter and Paul and the saltire cross of St Andrew are still clearly visible. On the wall below this is the handsome early classical memorial to Robert Pitcairn, post-Reformation commendator (administrator) of the abbey, archdeacon of St Andrews and Secretary of State from 1571 to 1583, who died in 1584.

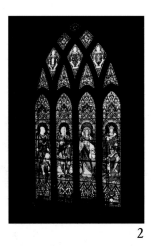

3

4

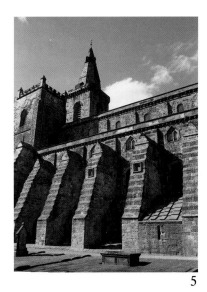

5

Further alterations chiefly aimed at strengthening the structure took place after the Reformation. The massive buttresses shoring up the aisles are dated 1620 on the south and 1625 on the north, and the south aisle vault was partly reconstructed at the same time. It may also have been that campaign that saw the outer walls of the galleries lowered and the roofs above them built to a steeper pitch, as shown on some early views of the abbey. But these last changes were reversed in the 1840s in a major operation of stabilisation, when three of the south arcade piers were also rebuilt and the present ceiling placed above the nave.

Close inspection of the masonry of the aisles reveals some evidence of the changes made after the Reformation to fit the nave for new patterns of worship. Above a number of the windows there are faint outlines of blocked windows which lit the timber galleries placed below the aisle vaults, and in the north aisle are traces of a handsome doorway of about 1700.

The Western Towers

The original western towers would have been massive structures which are unlikely to have risen as high as the existing north tower. They were probably capped by pyramidal roofs. Abbot Bothwell had to reconstruct the north tower in the later fifteenth century, but it was again reconstructed and given its fine spire by William Schaw, who died in 1602. In 1794 his imposing classical memorial was appropriately moved to the base of the tower he had rebuilt.

The south tower is an unworthy structure rebuilt in 1810 by William Stark, after the remains of the original collapsed in 1807. Eighteenth-century views of what had survived until then show that it had heavy pilasters with angle shafts at the corners, which would have been much more in keeping with the Romanesque structure. These views also show some evidence for the stubs of the west range of the cloister where it abutted the tower, although much of what remained of this range had been demolished in 1753.

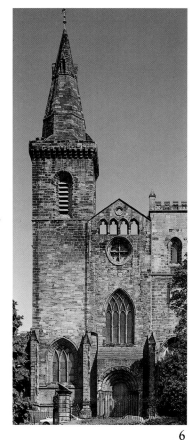

6

1. The arms of Abbot Richard de Bothwell.

2. The west window.

3. The north porch.

4. The 16th-century paintings on the vault at the east end of the north aisle.

5. The buttressing added to the south aisle in 1620.

6. The west front.

The Chapel of St Margaret and the New Choir

Queen Margaret was regarded as a saint by the Scots soon after her death in 1093, and it was much to the advantage of both the royal family and the abbey that this should be so. Her sanctity cast a reflected glory over the ruling dynasty which descended from her – many of whom were rather less holy! And the church which contained her remains became a place of pilgrimage, bringing considerable financial benefits through the offerings of the faithful at her tomb. In the mid-thirteenth century her remains were more splendidly housed, perhaps to accommodate the growing numbers of pilgrims.

An eastward extension of the monastic choir, ending in a flat eastern gable, with a lower chapel projecting beyond the central part, must have been nearing completion by 1249. On 18 August of that year Pope Innocent IV ruled that the church need not be newly consecrated, since the old walls remained largely as they were. From this it is evident that the main part of the choir was left unchanged within the extension. By June 1250 the new work was sufficiently complete for Margaret's body to be removed from its earlier grave in front of the screen separating the monks' choir from the nave (in which situation it had been in front of the high altar in the earlier church), to a shrine in the new eastern chapel. The body of her husband, Malcolm III, was also moved at the same time, apparently because it proved impossible to move one without the other.

The popularity of the shrine as a place of pilgrimage made further works necessary in 1368, when stones for it were bought in London at considerable expense. It was probably also the offerings of pilgrims which paid for the addition of a spacious Lady Chapel on the north side of the choir at an unknown date.

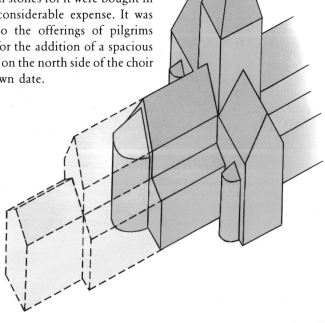

1. A sketch of the eastward extension of the abbey church in 1249.

2. An artist's impression of the shrine of Saint Margaret.

1

2

The only part of the medieval eastern limb to survive the early nineteenth-century construction of the new church is part of the lower walling of St Margaret's chapel. Little survived the collapse of the high gable of the choir in 1726, but what we have of the south and east walls is informative. The row of smaller bases shows there was a decorative wall arcade around the lower walls. In front of them the larger bases indicate that the space of the chapel was divided into two bays by wall shafts; these wall shafts would have carried the stone vaulting. Cut into the stone bench on which the wall arcade rested are basins in which the vessels used at the altars in the chapels were washed.

At the centre of the chapel was the shrine of the saint. The plinth, which survives, is composed of two steps of Frosterley 'marble', a stone from County Durham which could take a high polish. The shrine itself would have been of precious materials, and probably had a decorated timber cover which would only be lifted on important occasions – or for important pilgrims. By analogy with shrines elsewhere, it may have rested on an elaborate tomb-like base above the plinth, so elevating it sufficiently to be seen behind the high altar. Pilgrims had access to the shrine down the aisles of the choir, which were walled off from the choir itself.

The Monastic Buildings

xcept for any physical labour which might require them to be elsewhere in the greater precinct of the abbey, the Rule stipulated that the monks should spend their day within the enclosed world of the cloister, an open square around which the church and all the main domestic buildings were ranged. As was usual, at Dunfermline this was on the south side of the church, with lean-to covered walks around its perimeter. Most of the routine monastic activities, such as reading, copying or contemplation, were carried out in these covered walks. Nothing remains above ground of the ranges on the east and west sides of the cloister except for the ends adjacent to the surviving refectory, or eating hall, on the south. The monks' dormitory occupied the first floor of the east range, with their various day rooms and the chapter house below. One room of some importance in Scotland was the calefactory, or warming house, the only place in which the monks could enjoy a fire in the colder weather – and thus alleviate the hardship of living according to a Rule which had been written for inhabitants of southern Italy! This room was usually beneath the dormitory.

1. A block sketch of the monastic buildings.

2. The abbey from Pittencrieff Glen.

– – – The dashed line indicates the floor level of the principal buildings.
Those parts of the monastic complex that survive today.

KEY TO LETTERS

A Nave of abbey church

B Monks' choir

C Chapel of Saint Margaret's shrine

D Dormitory

E Chapter house

F Cloister

G West range

H Gatehouse

I Refectory (eating hall)

J Latrine

K Refectory undercroft

L Royal guesthouse

M Outer courtyard

N Inner precinct

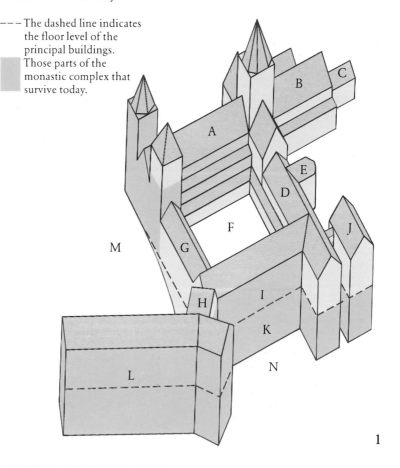

1

The ground floor of the west range was taken up with the provisions stores of the cellarer; on this side it was adjacent to the outer court of the precinct, where the community came into closest contact with the outside world, and where deliveries were received. Many buildings were grouped around the other sides of the outer court, including byres, stables, smithies and guest houses. The most magnificent of these guest houses still survives in part.

Access from the outer court to the inner parts of the abbey precinct was controlled by an impressive gatehouse. Apart from the abbey nave this is the most complete structure of the complex to have survived. Around the whole precinct was a stout wall intended for both privacy and defence, within which the monks moved about without risk of disturbance. Beyond the cloister were an infirmary, for old and sick monks, and residences for the abbot and perhaps also for the prior. Nothing survives of these, although to the north of the complex is a sixteenth-century building known as the Abbot's House. This may be on the site of the abbot's residence, although the first person firmly associated with the present building is Robert Pitcairn, appointed nominal commendator of the abbey after the Reformation in 1560. The cloister and monastic precinct were not built all in one operation. Indeed, a major abbey like Dunfermline was seldom entirely free from building works, with all the inconvenience and nuisance they caused.

The greatest disruption to the life of the abbey must have been caused in 1303, when Edward I of England ordered the domestic buildings to be destroyed, as part of his attempt to subdue Scotland to his will in the early stages of the Wars of Independence. Claims that not one stone was left upon another as a result were exaggerated, although it is clear that the monks were left without much of their living quarters. Extensive rebuilding was underway by 1329, when Robert I (the Bruce) made a contribution towards the construction of the refectory shortly before his death. Robert was buried before the high altar in the church on 9 June of that year, and a splendid marble tomb imported from Paris was erected over his body. Rebuilding of the great guest house in the outer court, and of the gatehouse between that and the refectory, eventually followed on, apparently at a considerably later period.

2

The Undercrofts of the Dormitory

The short stretch of the undercroft of the range on the east side of the cloister is difficult to understand, because the existence of the graveyard above it meant that only an L-shaped portion of it was excavated in 1920-4. It formed the lowest level of the range which included the monks' dormitory. Its architectural character, indicated by the windows of lancet shape and the traces of vaulting of the type known as sexpartite (with intermediate intersections), suggests it was probably built in the later decades of the thirteenth century. It appears to have escaped Edward I's destruction of 1303, at this lowest level at least.

Immediately to the east of, and running parallel to the dormitory undercroft, is a smaller block showing such close similarities to the dormitory that it must be contemporary with it. Since the block straddles the great drain it was evidently the reredorter, or latrine. The main latrine of the monks was on the same level as the dormitory, from which it would have been reached by some form of bridge, although a small latrine was also provided at the north end of the undercroft. The cubicles for the use of the monks would have been carried on a series of arches above the drain. Perhaps a little curiously to modern ideas of hygiene, the latrine basement is provided with a bread oven, at the back of a fireplace which has now lost its canopy.

1

The Refectory

The magnificence of Dunfermline as a monastic corporation is perhaps best demonstrated by the scale and grandeur of the refectory which was rebuilt around the 1320s, following its destruction by Edward I in 1303. Because of the fall of the land towards the south it was necessary to build a two-storeyed undercroft below the main dining hall, and the resulting south facade, with its strongly marked buttresses, is an awe-inspiring piece of architecture. Despite its destruction by the English king and its reconstruction for the fervently Scottish Robert I, the architectural details are still essentially English-inspired, although the elaborate tracery of the extraordinary seven-light west window may suggest that the English sources were not altogether understood.

1. The undercrofts of the dormitory and latrine.

2. The window lighting the refectory pulpit.

3. A detail of the refectory's west window.

4. An artist's impression of the refectory.

2

3

4

The dining hall on the level of the cloister was covered by a timber ceiling. Along each flank were tall two-light windows, except at the eastern end, where the raised dais of the high table was accentuated by a three-light window. Beside the high table on the south side was the pulpit. Externally, this is carried on an arch between two buttresses, and it is lit by a pair of narrow two-light windows with corresponding arches towards the interior.

The lower storeys of the range were each covered by two aisles of stone vaulting carried on a central row of columns. The excellent state of preservation of the internal lower walling, which was only re-excavated in 1920-4, enables us still to see incised lines which may have been connected with the setting-out and construction of the vaults. The lowest storey could be reached either by a stair within the entrance to the refectory from the cloister, or by doorways from the outside. Access to the middle floor had to be altered when the adjoining gatehouse was rebuilt to its present form. One door was created from within the gateway itself and, in addition, a corridor from the first-floor chamber of the gate was projected out on arches between the buttresses. But the main access was probably from the east side of the cloister, and a chamber with a fine vault and traceried window, directly below the refectory dais, appears to have acted as a vestibule of some importance. Its window was linked with a canopy above the door at the lowest level.

The Gatehouse

Although this gate has doorways leading into the ranges to either side, it certainly was not built to its present form until after the refectory had been completed. On the side of the gate facing the inner precinct, for example, the arch is rather awkwardly keyed into a buttress of the refectory, whilst the masonry at the higher level is not bonded into the buttress at all. On architectural grounds it seems unlikely that the gate was built much before the fifteenth century, though there was probably a gatehouse here from the beginning. Because of its situation on a steeply sloping site, the gate had to be given a rather irregular shape, with vaults at two levels covering the carriageway which runs through it.

Immediately above the carriageway are chambers at two levels. That above the inner part of the gate is finer than its counterpart to the west, and is covered by a vault with 'tierceron' (additional) ribs. It may have been intended to serve as a vestibule to the refectory, through which the food was brought from the kitchen on the other side of the road running through the gate. The room above the outer part of the gate was apparently reached by an external timber staircase.

On the top floor of the gatehouse is a single rectangular chamber, vaulted in two bays, and now reached by a modern timber stair. The fine quality of the room, with its large canopied fireplace, suggests that it was occupied by one of the more important office holders of the abbey, although in some monasteries the upper floor of the gate was used as a courthouse. Above this chamber was a defensible wall head with a parapet carried on corbels (projecting stones), and there may have been another room within the roof which once covered the whole structure.

The precinct of the abbey is said to have been surrounded by a wall 3,000 feet long, but only a few fragments of it survive. The one significant relic is part of another of the gates into the precinct on St Margaret Street. It was known as the 'Nethir Yet' or South Port, but was largely demolished in 1751.

1. The gatehouse from the east.
2. The gatehouse from the north west.
3. The abbey from the royal guest house.
4. The royal guest house.

1

2

3

The Guest House

This is one of the most intriguing – and certainly one of the most complex – parts of the entire abbey. A great abbey was expected to provide hospitality for all who called on it, although the scale of that hospitality was in proportion with the importance of the visitor. The abbey's founder and his successors were particularly important visitors and, since Dunfermline was a royal foundation, it is likely that a guest house conceived on such a princely scale as that we now see was for royal use only. Accommodation for others was probably in less magnificent hostels around the outer court.

The construction of the royal guest house may have begun in the earlier fourteenth century, along with the refectory; however, there is now little in its architecture which appears earlier than the fifteenth century. The most dramatic view of the guest house is from the glen to its south, where the steep drop required the erection of walls of dramatic height. It is also from this side that the complexity of the building is most apparent. Apart from obvious changes in window types, there are significant changes in the details of the angled base courses, suggesting that the great length of the range was only achieved by degrees.

4

As it now stands, the earliest part of this range is probably the central portion, running westwards from the south-western angle of the gatehouse. Although greatly modified since first built, this part was originally covered at basement level by two aisles of vaulting extending for seven bays. Above this the main space had five large windows embraced internally by handsomely moulded arches.

1

To its west is a large first-floor kitchen, above an undercroft vaulted in two aisles. Nothing in this kitchen block appears to be earlier than the last years of the fifteenth century. But in view of its position between the refectory and the royal guest house, it may be a rebuilding of an earlier main kitchen. The kitchen itself is slightly larger than its undercroft, because it was carried outwards on arches between the buttresses. Around its walls was a variety of fireplaces of different sizes and dates of construction.

The section of the guest house range at the opposite end from the kitchen may have been added or rebuilt soon after the kitchen, because it has a fireplace at first-floor level of a type usually datable to around 1500. It was originally unlike the rest of the range in having no stone vaults over its basement, and vaults were only added as part of an extensive later remodelling.

2

The Abbey and The Reformation

3

The initial spiritual fervour of Dunfermline, as at many of the older monasteries, had probably waned long before the Reformation. By 1559 there were no more than 25 monks in the house. Towards the end a less dedicated way of life was also fostered by the absence of proper leadership, because from 1500 Dunfermline, like many other abbeys, was headed by commendators and not by monastic abbots. Commendators were usually royal appointees granted a religious house as a reward for their services, and few of them showed any great interest in monastic life. Indeed, as the wind of reform came to blow through Scotland's Church, the main concern of many of them was to obtain as much as possible of their abbey's possessions for their families. Dunfermline has the unenviable record of being the Scottish monastery with the longest unbroken run of being ruled by commendators. The first was James Stewart, a brother of James IV and archbishop elect of St Andrews, appointed in 1500, although, even before that, in 1491 an attempt had been made to grant the abbey to an Italian cardinal.

Monastic life came to an end in the first waves of the Reformation. By 1559 the furnishings associated with the old forms of worship had been destroyed by the Lords of the Congregation, and in 1560 the buildings were sacked. As early as 1563 the eastern parts were roofless and tumbling, and the nave also was showing signs of collapse. The continuing use of the latter as a parish church, however, meant that efforts were soon made to bring it back into repair.

Also in Dunfermline's favour was the continuing interest shown by royalty. In 1587 James VI passed an Act of Annexation by which he attempted to reclaim as much Church property as he could for the Crown. Although most of Dunfermline's vast estates were already alienated, a considerable proportion was retained by the Crown. In 1589 James VI granted this to his queen, Anne of Denmark, and she ordered the remodelling of the royal guest house as a palace for herself.

By the time that work started on the palace preliminary repairs had already been made to the abbey nave in 1570, under the direction of Sir Robert Drummond. William Schaw, probably on the queen's bidding, reconstructed the upper part of the north-west tower with its spire. In 1602 Schaw was buried in the nave. On the queen's orders a fine monument was raised to his memory and this now stands beneath the tower he rebuilt.

1. The kitchen.

2. An artist's impression of the royal guest house.

3. "Four Evangelists Stoning the Pope", painted by Giroliamo Da Treviso (1535). *(Reproduced by Gracious Permission of Her Majesty the Queen)*

4. The memorial in the nave to Robert Pitcairn, commendator (administrator) of the abbey after the Reformation.

4

The Royal Palace

 In the course of the operation to adapt the guest house as a palace for Queen Anne of Denmark, her Master of Works, William Schaw, made extensive changes. The windows of the main floor of the central part of the range were remodelled to rectangular form, the western portion of the range was almost completely rebuilt, and a upper storey was either added along the whole range, or rebuilt so completely as to leave no trace of what had been there before.

1

1. King Charles I as a young man, painted by Robert Peake.
   (National Galleries of Scotland)

2. Queen Anne of Denmark, painted by Paul Van Somer.

3. An artist's impression of the royal bedchamber.

2

The arrangement of windows and cross walls suggests that the palace consisted of a servery next to the retained kitchen, followed by a hall of four bays, and a chamber of three bays. The chamber was given a delightful projecting central window where the queen might sit and look over the gardens in the glen below. Could this have been the room in which the queen gave birth to the future Charles I in 1600? Above it was another spacious chamber, whilst above the hall and servery area there was a single long room. This was probably a gallery for exercise in bad weather, and must have afforded fine views across the surrounding countryside. Along the gallery small projecting oriel windows provided attractive sitting-out areas.

Despite its magnificence the palace had a relatively short life. The last recorded major repairs to it were made in anticipation of a visit by Charles I in 1633.

3

The Abbey in Recent Times

Between the seventeenth and nineteenth centuries attempts were made to shore up those parts of the abbey church still in use and to adapt them for reformed worship. But the rest of the complex rapidly decayed. In 1672 part of the ruined choir was blown down; the east gable itself fell in 1726, and in 1753 the great central tower fell — though fortunately away from the nave. The nave was more directly affected when the massive remains of the south-western tower fell during a violent storm on 19 August 1807. It was replaced by the inappropriately flimsy structure designed by William Stark we now see.

A turning point in the history of the abbey church came with the decision to build a new church for the parish on the site of the original eastern limb. The architect William Burn prepared designs in 1817, and the foundation stone was laid in the following year. The new church was opened for worship on 30 September 1821. Regrettably, no adequate record was made of what still survived of the medieval eastern limb before it was destroyed, although in the course of the work human remains considered to be those of King Robert the Bruce were found. They were re-interred on 5 November 1819 below the position later occupied by the pulpit.

On completion of the new building responsibility for the maintenance of the nave and the remains of St Margaret's chapel was assumed by the state. Plans for the drastic restoration of the nave, which were to include the insertion of an imita-tion vault in plaster, were drawn up by William Burn in 1820, but were rejected. Instead, the important decision was taken to preserve the nave essentially in its medieval condition. Major repairs were undertaken between 1847 and 1849, involv-ing the replacement of roofs, the re-opening of blocked windows and the repair of damage caused by the insertion of galleries. These left the nave in much the condition we now see. Other works since then have included the exposure of the south-east processional door in 1905, the excavation of the earlier church beneath the nave floor in 1916 and the excavation of the lower levels of the refectory and dormitory blocks in 1920-4. The abbey can now be enjoyed as one of the most ambitious — and most complete — groups of buildings for a religious community to have been raised in medieval Scotland.

Illustration: *Royal Commission on Ancient Monuments, Scotland*